LIVE

ALIGNED

WITH THE REAL YOU

How To Better Understand Yourself and Others

Faith Deeter, MFT

Lustre Publishing
Santa Ynez, California

Cover Photo: Faith and Lucero 1991
            Courtesy of Nancy Canter

ISBN: 978-0-9818192-1-1

Printed in the United States of America.

For Donald

Acknowledgements

This book was made possible by the encouragement and support of so many. Thank you all.

CONTENTS

Then...

Faith and Fifo 1992

And now...

Faith, Fifo, and Fancy 2008

Prologue

Alignment is a simple way to better understand yourself, and it is a simple way to better understand others. As you read each chapter, I hope you will come to have a greater sense as to why you do what you do, and more understanding as to why other people may be doing what they're doing.

When it comes to feeling satisfied in life or making any sort of lasting change, it's been my experience that what helps the most is a solid understanding that all the parts of a person must act in unison in order to make change that lasts.

We are like a symphony with many voices that harmonize together – or not. This book is meant to help you discover which part or parts of yourself may need realigning and which part or parts may be perfectly aligned already.

Chapter one is my own story about discovering alignment completely by accident through a life-threatening experience. Chapter two is how I lost the alignment and how I rediscovered the concept through conscientious searching. Chapters three through seven review each part of alignment individually and chapter eight brings them all together.

I believe we are each put here to be ourselves. I hope this book makes it a little easier to do so.

1

DISCOVERY

I'm not sure why I pulled off my shoes before sliding over the glossy, smooth back of the white stallion. It just seemed like the thing to do. The white prom dress I was wearing was arranged in huge ruffles around me. I moved my horse, Lucero, into the surf and galloped, hair streaming, over the wet sand while salt water sprayed and his hooves splashed and pounded.

My mother took photos. The next day, I would cut off my hair and keep it. Unlike others had before me, I would not lose mine. I would cut it and keep it before I would lose it. But today, I would not think of any of these things. In this moment, gliding along the glistening shoreline in the sun, I felt happy and free.

It was a time in my life when things were crystal clear and for a short time, I knew the meaning of my life. I knew what mattered to me and I knew what didn't. I knew my capabilities and I knew my limitations. I knew exactly what I wanted to do and nothing and no one could stop me from doing it. No risk was too great. No embarrassment too daunting. No cost too high. In fact, there was no cost in doing things; there was only cost in not doing them.

I had catapulted almost instantly to a place where the rules had changed and life mattered in an entirely different way because, at twenty years old, I learned I might not have more than a few months left to live. Suddenly, I had lymphatic cancer and with that knowledge, my entire perspective and willingness clicked into new alignment. Cancer became my spring board.

In hind sight, and since I have recovered fully, the alarm of imminent death has turned out to have been a great gift for propulsion for living. When juxtaposed against death itself, fears that I had allowed to limit me, were gone. In fact, what I believed to have been limits turned out to have been mirage-like illusions that had actually never been limits at all. What a surprise it was to find out that so much of what I'd thought mattered in life, simply didn't matter.

What others thought of me was no longer relevant. My accomplishments were important only from the stand-point that I hoped I would one day be well enough to once again do the things I loved. I dared to do things I never would have done before, because time all of the sudden mattered. Time mattered, other people mattered, and for

2

the first time in my life, I understood just how much I mattered.

But why I mattered was the surprising thing. Bald and waif-like, I was no longer beautiful. Weak and weary, I was no longer athletic. Drugged and bedraggled, my memory was so impaired it felt like a dream that I had ever been smart. By the end of the treatments I was so weak that getting from the bedroom to the kitchen was an event. Compared with what I had been able to achieve just a few months prior, I was essentially useless so why I mattered turned out to be a simple and pleasant surprise.

I mattered only because I was alive and for no other reason than I was me and alive. I was the only Faith that would ever live and the only one that could fulfill the unique potential of my life. When I was young, my piano teacher referred to me often as her 'unlimited potential gal' and ill, weak, and weary though I was, I felt like I finally understood the potential innately available within me; potential I did not have to earn and potential that would never go away despite my circumstances.

The simple and profound gift came in knowing that my primary purpose in life was to simply be Faith, and to truly be Faith what I had to do was be real; be on the outside who I really was on the inside, and the rest would simply unfold. Compared with death, being real was surprisingly easy. Whether in public or on my own, I did what was right for me.

I was in college. It was time to register for class which meant standing in three hour lines that stretched outside the building. When standing and waiting became too exhausting I sat on the ground; and when getting up and down to move forward in the line had become too tiring, I tossed my backpack ahead of me and scooted.

To get my books, I crawled around the floor of the university book store and the fact that others looked on in uncomfortable glances didn't bother me at all. I didn't care about anything other than getting done what I wanted to do. My mother offered to help me but I refused to let her. What I cared about that day was holding onto the last few bits of independence and self-control I still had.

Over time, I recovered. My body slowly strengthened and within a year I was completely well – at least physically. I got on with things. I got back to life, and like the cancer I had just eliminated from my body, life slowly got back to me.

I went to graduate school. I went to graduate school because after graduating college, I wasn't sure what to do next. What I knew was that I loved where I lived – a tiny, rural, picturesque place with a tourism-based industry, the Santa Ynez Valley. I had a horse and what I really wanted to do was ride my horse; have a place to live, and earn enough money for groceries. Now home from college with my Bachelor's degree, it seemed like my only choices for work were the same as when I'd left; become a waitress or work in a gift shop unless I went back to school.

Back to school is where I went. An English major before, this time I studied Psychology. The curriculum I found in December would start in January. "Well, here I go," I thought to myself; "I'll just jump right in." After asking my parents if I could move home to keep costs down, and armed with a student loan, I started studying.

All went well until I took a simple elective – The Psychology of Women. What I thought would be an enlightening class about feminine something or other turned out to be, in my opinion, a class teaching that women are victimized by men, victimized by society, and in one way or another, always victims. Victims? It seemed an incredible concept and given my recent experience, sounded to me like nails on a chalk board. With bodies that work, minds that remember, and a digestive tract that digests their food? Women have voices and choices and the ability to act.

"You mean women don't like the choices they sometimes are required to make?" I queried.

"Sometimes women do not have choices," was the reply.

It became a duel of sorts. The teacher said, "If a woman is in a class and her male instructor is making derogatory comments toward women, the woman can't do anything about it."

"She could ask him to stop," I suggested.

"But he could fail her. He is the instructor and he holds the power."

"He doesn't hold her power and if she thinks so, she is simply not using what is hers. If it bothers her that much, she could go above him and talk to the Dean. If that doesn't work she could go to the School Board. If she really wanted to, she could go to the media, not that any person would want to do that, but certainly the only thing stopping her would be herself. Either that, or she could simply change her mind about what she found demeaning. That choice might be the most powerful choice of all."

I could not sit silently and accept what felt to me to be a travesty unfolding before my eyes. Here was a woman who seemed to be categorically including all women in her belief system, who seemed to want to define me and my life by her beliefs as well. I would not agree.

Victimization, a complex and complicated topic, was much deeper than this class was willing to explore. I had sat in waiting rooms with women who had agreed to have their breasts removed, with men who had agreed to have their testicles removed, with people who had lost their ovaries, their uterus', parts of their colon, both young and old who had consented to have poison injected into their bodies in the hope of becoming well.

These were people who could have easily considered themselves victims but every person I had met had made a decision not to be one. If these people would not hand their power over to a villain as unpredictable and lethal as cancer, I could not agree that an objectionable comment made by a male professor in front of a female student was a more valid reason to do so.

In hindsight, I imagine my teacher hadn't known what to do with me. I had an answer for everything; and true to myself as I was at the time, I didn't hold back.

"If you live in a dangerous neighborhood, move. If you don't have money to move, get in a car and drive away. If you don't have a car but you still have legs, run. Would you say you can't move if you knew a hurricane was coming in two hours to blow you away? What if a fire were coming? Would you say you can't move?"

I knew that sometimes the choices we have to choose from are limited. Sometimes we don't like the options and every alternative may seem equally bad, but I also knew that when something was important enough, if a person had enough at stake, like their life – they could take action as required, regardless of the potential cost.

I also knew that if a person told themselves they couldn't move, then something else was more important to them than moving. Perhaps they feared the cost of moving would be greater than the cost of staying, and maybe it would be. But if that person was not honest that staying was actually a choice, they might pretend to themselves that they had no choice.

As long as there is air in our lungs, we can still do something, even if that something is as simple as changing our mind about things. Concentration camp survivor Viktor Frankl said, "Man's final freedom is to choose his own way." There is always a choice.

With responsibility and ownership, comes power. I have never believed that we create all of our circumstances, but we always have the power to choose our response. It's not that I was trying to be harsh or insensitive. I had seen injustice, judgment, and unfairness and I didn't like it. Feeling powerless is a horrible way to feel.

I have never forgotten a homeless man I met when I was sick. We both waited in the parking lot outside a hospital emergency room. Although I couldn't know for sure, it seemed he was kept outside because he was homeless and for no other reason than that.

My white blood cell count had fallen to zero, and I was advised to not sit amongst the people in the waiting room for the two hours it took to get me admitted. A virus could have proven to be as life threatening as the immobilized colon that had distended my belly and that later nearly ruptured. Instead of inside, I sat in the cold, dark parking lot, my insides paralyzed by chemotherapy drugs, in the worst pain I could ever image feeling – worse than the bone marrow biopsy I had experienced weeks prior.

The homeless man waiting in the parking lot was highly distressed, too. Pacing around, he told me how worried he was about his friend inside who had been stabbed. When the nurse came to give him an update, she was coarse and abrupt with him. The homeless man asked to see his friend. The nurse said no. Even in my pain, or perhaps because of my pain, I could relate to the pain of this other human being, who like me was alone and afraid.

"The man inside is my friend," he said to me. We were
no different, this homeless man and I. I had a home, he
didn't, but we each were human and knew what it was to
have fear. Pain is pain and everyone matters.

But pain or fear of it, excruciating and immobilizing as
it can be, could not be allowed to dictate my outcome that
day. The doctors, not realizing that my intestines were
paralyzed, surmised that I was constipated from the
medications and provided me with a gallon jug of liquid
called, "Go lightly" that I drank as quickly as I could.

When that didn't resolve my problem, they gave me a
second gallon. The doctors went home for the night and
the nurses refused any pain medication. Within hours, I
was in even worse shape than before and still worsening.

My mother was with me but neither one of us could get
the nurses to believe the urgency of my situation. When I
could no longer withhold crying, the tears only seemed to
make it more difficult for the nurses to hear the validity of
my complaints.

"My God," I thought. "They think I'm over-reacting
and I'm supposed to sit here and be a good patient while
they let me die." My mother knew me. She got it.

"Call someone else," I told her. "Call anybody who will
listen."

Having seen doctors at Stanford University Hospital in
Palo Alto, my mother dialed them. The answering service
took her message. Several minutes passed. No call back.
"Call again, do whatever it takes, but tell them that I am
going to burst and then I'm going to die." I knew it as

certainly as I knew the sun would rise that next morning and, if something didn't happen fast, I knew I wouldn't be alive to see it.

The doctor my mother finally reached around 2 am yelled at her for her persistence but he heard what she was telling him and within minutes I was whisked away in a wheel chair. Before I knew it, I had an x-ray, a doctor, a surgeon, tubes shoved in various places to vacuum away pressure, and thankfully, finally, morphine.

It was an important lesson in being willing to act in accordance with myself even when the experts were telling me I was wrong. It was an important lesson in being willing to upset other people, disregard authority, and reject protocol. When your guts are screaming, "You're gonna die," it pays to listen to your guts.

Too often in the past, I had shut off emotionally, refused to listen, and refused to act because acting in accordance with my gut instinct was scary, unfamiliar, and might upset other people. I'd been raised by good parents to be a good person and obey life's systems and authority, but I was finally learning, as was my mother, that there is sometimes a time and place to say, "No." It was this life experience and perspective that I carried forward with me to my Psychology of Women class. Time and time again, I just couldn't keep my mouth shut.

I don't recall the exact wording of the teacher's comments on the class journal I was required to write but they were something very close to, "I am concerned about you becoming a therapist. You are dangerous." The label stung. There were also words of caution that she would fail me if I didn't learn my lessons better.

I had a choice. I took action. I changed my grading option from a standard grade to a pass or fail so I wouldn't lose my straight A grade point average and had a meeting with the dean. As I had completed all of my assignments, I couldn't imagine the teacher would fail me. She didn't. I passed the class and went on with my education, but that teacher's comment was burned in my mind like a brand on cattle. When you are real, Faith, people may find you dangerous, and perhaps you should be concerned about that.

Dangerous was a word I had never heard used in connection with myself before. I was used to words like friendly, nice, maybe even shy. The neighbor whose pool I sometimes swam in as a child commented that my smile was so big and permanent that when I would go under the water smiling and come up the same, she was amazed and somewhat relieved that I hadn't drowned. Dangerous was a word I couldn't fathom.

I did realize at the time that I was powerful. I was powerful because I was honest. I was powerful because I refused to censor anything I had to say and I was willing to say anything and do just about anything because with the idea of no life left to live, I had nothing to lose except body parts. That is truly how I looked at things at the time, nothing to lose but body parts and plenty to gain.

The teacher was not the only one that made an impression as I got back to life. I don't recall who it was that described the following scenario, "When one person's thinking gets too far from other people's thinking, no one can relate to them anymore. It's like one person is traveling in a hot air balloon while others are traveling along the ground."

"Great," I thought. "So what you're telling me is that unless I change back to the way I was, I will be alone." It wasn't that I was trying to change or not trying to change. All I was trying to do was go forward with my life.

Having finished school, I found a job and got out on my own. Things moved along and, over time, life's pressures somehow caught up with me. I found myself feeling overwhelmed with the pressures of living.

No longer outspoken, I was often silent. No longer energetic, I preferred to be still. I was tired, in fact I was exhausted. Looking in the mirror several years later, I hardly recognized who was looking back. The pressures of life came seeping back and the power I'd embraced slowly ebbed away.

"What happened to her?" I wondered. "What happened to that adventurous spirit and smile?" The horse I'd planned my career around riding, sat in the corral unridden. I didn't know where the person I'd finally found had gone. All I knew was the one who had galloped barefoot and bareback through the ocean didn't seem to be there anymore. It was as if my soul had become vacant and my spirit had lost its force.

DISCOVERY

Somehow, in getting better physically, I had lost touch with me. But one day I had a mind to get myself back. It was better to try than to die; or live a lie.

2

REDISCOVERY

I was taking a shower when I felt it. The water was wet and for the first time in years, I actually felt the wetness of the water. I had known it was wet, of course, but the heat and the steam and the feel of it sliding over my skin had somehow escaped my attention. I'd been so busy with other things. How long had it been since I'd actually felt the feel of the water, I wondered.

I had spent my adult years attempting to build the life I felt I was supposed to create. I was building a business, making a home, having a relationship, and accumulating the things I believed would bring me security and happiness. I went to bed each night and got up each morning with an increasing sense of dread at the never ending items on my to-do list. My life was moving in one big circle and though the circle was widening over time, I was going nowhere.

The bills came in a circle. Meals each day were a circle. Sleeping and waking up was a circle. Driving to work and home again was a circle. The weeks turned into months and the months into years and each day was nearly the same circle as the one before. Eventually, I succeeded in accumulating the things.

I had a profession that worked. I owned my home. I had great friends but not enough time to spend with them. All the things I had worked to achieve were here and now I worked to maintain them. I did the yard work and the laundry, paid the bills, and went to the office. I pulled the weeds and did the dishes, always behind and busy taking care of things but not taking care of me. Where was I in my life?

When I read in a book that our home is a reflection of us, I wanted to cry. Mine was big, old, had a gigantic yard, an ancient pool, and was decomposing around me. I was working like crazy to fix it up yet things broke more quickly than I could repair them and money was a constant factor. If the house was meant to be a reflection of me, then I was in breakdown. Indeed, I was in breakdown but it felt like it was because of the house and the responsibilities of my life, not vice versa.

I resented the statement that the house was a reflection of me. What was that supposed to mean? If you have a perfect house, you're perfect? What it meant to me was that I was in over my head and struggling to hang on by my fingernails, which incidentally, I chewed. It also meant that according to the books I'd read, I didn't measure up.

15

In an attempt to be helpful, a few close friends suggested I sell the house. I didn't want to sell it. I wanted to make it beautiful, the way I knew it could be, if only I knew how.

My retired next door neighbor mowed his grass every three days on a ride on mower. His yard never grew a weed. Whenever I could, I would push my ancient mower through the grass, the drive train would slip, the bag would detach and I would end up blasted in the face with grass cuttings as I hurriedly bent to re-secure the bag.

Asking for advice from my wise-appearing neighbor, he tried to be consoling and assured me that the way to eat an elephant was one bite at a time. The problem was, my elephant was eating me. I was being swallowed by my life and I was drowning. I discovered what anxiety attacks feel like and also depression. Every day I felt like giving up. Some days, I went back to bed and did.

I was hiding. I hid from the neighbors who walked by my unfinished yard each morning and hid from the mail that accumulated in a stack. I hid from my horse that I felt guilty about not riding. I hid from many of my friends. I was fortunate in so many ways and yet, I was miserable.

There were so many expectations coming from so many sources that collided. I was trying to do things right, but right was subjective. Out of school and in the real world, there was no single person available to stamp my life with a passing grade. It took more than reading a textbook and putting down correct answers to feel that I was doing well.

The fact that I could do Geometry, understand cell division, and find all the nouns in a sentence didn't help me manage my life. I knew what I wanted but I didn't know how to get there. While I logically understood the concept that the only opinion that truly mattered was mine, emotionally I felt bombarded by external messages that I was failing.

Better Homes and Garden Magazine showed lovely gardens and beautiful interiors. Magazines at the grocery check-out showed how to have a flat stomach in ten days. Everywhere I looked, I saw expectations, and looking at my own reflection and the reflection of my environment, it was clear to me that I didn't rate. What had happened to not caring about what anyone else might think? What happened to knowing that being a good person, keeping food on the table, and a roof over my head was enough?

When one of my closest friends was twenty-seven years old, she jumped off a bridge and killed herself. The terrifying thing was that I felt I understood why. We had been friends since we were nine years old and were so much alike, we could have been sisters. Both bright and likable, there were high expectations for us and our future. I was upset with my friend for what she'd done. I was sad, and missed her; but I wasn't one of the people who said, why would someone with everything going for her do something like that?

In my twenties, I ended a flawed relationship with a person I dearly loved and whom my family adored. It wasn't something I wanted to do, but no matter how much we tried or loved each other, it seemed we simply could not get along.

After some time, I began a relationship with someone else. Unlike the choice I had made in my prior relationship, this time I selected a person with whom I got along better. He was steady, good-natured, and kind so when I heard from my family that he was a loser, I was confused.

I don't recall my family ever asking me why I'd made the choice I had or if I was happy. No one seemed to care that we were friends or that he had been willing to help me rescue hundreds of fish from ankle deep slime when the canal that they lived in was drained. They didn't put any value on the fact that he had hot dinner waiting for me when I came home from work, that he never yelled or pressured me, or that he, too, struggled to find his way in the world.

I felt under attack by the very people I expected would support me. Just a few years prior, my parents would have done anything for me but now my family made their feelings quite clear. I had not chosen according to correct criteria and the underlying message from them was stated outright, even to people in the grocery store; I was stupid.

"I'm the same person I've always been," I wanted to shout. Although I've never been much of a drinker, on Thanksgiving Day I sat on my back patio with a bottle of wine and drank it until I decided I could be "too sick" to attend the family dinner. I turned even further inward and felt more and more alone. Here I was, as usual, trying to do the best back-flips I could manage, and instead of the applause I anticipated and needed, I was dodging tomatoes.

In a sense, their criticism caused me to rely even more heavily on the relationship and it impaired my ability to accurately evaluate it for myself. While all the good things about it were true, rather than bringing me closer to myself, the relationship brought with it a whole new realm of responsibilities, complications, and distractions because it included the needs of another human being. I could barely take care of myself.

The one and only place I could depend on finding sanctuary was with my horse. It had been that way as long as I could remember. At nine, I got my first pony. Before that, I rode plastic Breyer brand toy horses around the floor of my bedroom. Now it was Fifo, a massively boned thoroughbred mare, who was my magic carpet to a special place.

From the moment my boot went into the stirrup iron and I swung into the saddle, I found myself in the same internal location again and again, a place of rightness. Regardless of the terrain or circumstance, I was in the moment and able to act or react to stay in rhythm with my mount and my surroundings. Even when things didn't go smoothly, I didn't unravel. Time took a different pace. Life was right and so was I.

There were plenty of problems while riding but none of that mattered. There were hazards to deal with: holes, wire, other animals, and wind. Deer came crashing through the bushes sounding like a predator coming. Fifo could spin on her haunches in seconds and being an ex-race horse, she could go from zero to sixty in a flash.

One day while riding through a river, Fifo tripped. Struggling to regain her footing, she clambered against the unstable river rocks until ultimately losing the battle, we were both sprawling head long into the water. Now drenched and soaking, legs trembling, we each got up as quickly as we could. Loose, Fifo sped forward to run home and just as suddenly stopped. It was clear to me instinct told her to run but she didn't leave.

Sloshing my way to her, I followed the rule that every horseman lives by: "As long as you and your horse are not injured and it's safe to do so, when you fall off, get back on." We continued on our journey without further incident and actually, had a wet, wonderful ride.

Why could I not react that way to my life in general, I wondered. I didn't take the fall as a failure or anything other than something that had just happened. I didn't panic. I didn't give up. I didn't walk home being too afraid to ride on. I didn't worry about what others would think, and I didn't have the vet out to do unneeded research to find something defective with my horse or with me. We fell. We were fine. We got up. We went on. It was as simple as that.

So when the bag would fall off the lawn mower or my family did not approve, why did I feel I was such a failure then? My whole life had become centered around an attempt to generate security and approval. I tried to create it through my relationship, my home, my career, money, and even when I generated results in these areas, I still didn't find it. Yet, in what is considered a most dangerous and unpredictable setting, horseback riding, I felt the safest, happiest, and most secure.

It was while galloping full speed through a ploughed field that it occurred to me that when I have the least amount of traditional security, I feel the most joy. The saddle does not come with a seat belt, and the mistake of tying oneself to a saddle is, in fact, the most dangerous and potentially life-threatening of errors.

Generating security in the traditional sense never did bring the allure of promised safety nor did it bring the freedom I was yearning for. The word itself implies securing, locking, barring, done by security guards in maximum security prisons. Life is not safe. I realized then that true security could only come from inside of me.

Riding is what consistently transported me to the place I wanted to be. I wanted to bring that place back with me to the rest of my life. Always a thinker, I thought of it often. What had I had, and what had I lost, from my life before? Then one day, I heard the term 'structural integrity' and those two words were an epiphany.

Structural integrity related to buildings. A building was said to be in structural integrity when it stood straight up and down, in alignment and balance with its foundation. It was said to be out of integrity, if any part of it did not line up with the part below. I pictured a sky scraper, tall, straight, reaching for the sky and then suddenly, the sky scraper had a head on it and a smiley face. Right then, it occurred to me that I could be balanced and in alignment just like a building. I, too, could have structural integrity.

The words gave me a picture and the picture was a map. From that day forward I began to work on the map. I knew that people were made up of thoughts, feelings, words, and actions. Each part might be a block of the building and while I had thought of people in terms of these parts before, I had never envisioned the parts being connected or inner-related as I suddenly realized they were.

If structural integrity for buildings meant the building would stand straight up and down from a foundation, then structural integrity for people would be the ability to think, feel, speak, and act aligned straight up and down from a foundation, too.

As I identified each block, I was delighted to discover that the picture was simple. I had a guide for myself as a whole person that made sense and I didn't need a PhD or a dictionary to understand it.

How weary I had grown of reading self-help books that provided great principles which I didn't know how to apply. While the books presented helpful information, the ideas didn't stick. The block man, however, stuck with me like a skewer. It was like a rod or a bolt of lightning that once inside my brain, wouldn't get out. I began seeing alignment and misalignment everywhere I looked.

My mom had a disagreement with my sister. "Look," I exclaimed. Right there at the table, I began scribbling on a napkin. "This is what's happening." I drew the picture. "You are both out of alignment." I remember the astonishment on my mother's face as she saw the pieces coming together and the relief.

"That's amazing," she said, "That actually makes sense."

I began listening differently to the stories told to me in my counseling office. Like me, I discovered that most other people did not tend to think of themselves in terms of a whole picture made up of inner-related parts. They might think of their actions or their feelings without considering how those corresponded with their thoughts or beliefs.

The more I paid attention, the more I learned that when thoughts, feelings, words, and actions do not align, lasting change is nearly impossible. Whichever block or blocks were misaligned would cause the others to misalign as well. Not only was the picture helping me to be more gentle and patient with myself, I found myself becoming more understanding and compassionate with those around me. All of us, it seemed, shifted in and out of alignment at various times, and in various places of our lives.

It wasn't long before I discovered that my epiphany wasn't new at all. It had been known for ages. Gandhi said, "Happiness is when what you think, what you say, and what you do are in harmony;" but, until I had the picture, even words as powerful as his had gone in one ear and out the other. Alignment is what many of the great teachers of the world had been teaching. Some called it self-actualization and there were other names, but it wasn't until I got the picture, that I finally got the picture. The picture looked like this.

There are five blocks stacked one on top of the other. The blocks have a head on top and arms: a block person. The bottom block is self. The next block is thoughts. The third block is feelings. The forth block is words. The top block is action. When the blocks stack straight up and down, the person is in alignment.

When any block does not line up with the one beneath, the person becomes crooked like a spine in need of a chiropractic adjustment.

I noticed that when I was out of alignment, I felt weakened, less stable, and unbalanced just like the picture showed me. I also felt depressed, anxious, irritable, and tired. My actions became one big strategy to avoid whatever I felt unable to handle or to avoid feelings I didn't want to feel.

It was only when I understood how to realign each part of myself, in unison, that I felt in integrity. It was a thrilling epiphany and I recognized the place. It was a place quite similar to the one I had known during my illness. I also discovered that it was my alignment, or rather my misalignment, that was beneath all my surface issues.

In the past, I hadn't known what to do to right myself but now I did know what to do. I could move myself from where I was to where I wanted to be. The goal was to get the inside of me back to the outside of my life through my thoughts, feelings, words, and actions. My new map showed me how.

When we are
aligned…

Words that align with
self will tend to be
positive words.

Thoughts match self. If
we are a kind person,
out thoughts will
believe we are a kind
person.

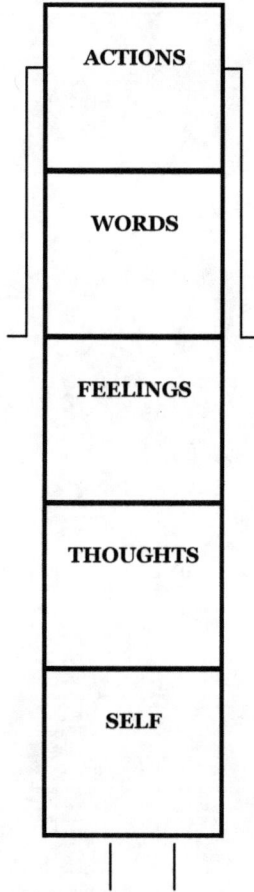

ACTIONS

WORDS

FEELINGS

THOUGHTS

SELF

Actions that align with
self will reflect our
values. If we are a kind
person, we will do kind
actions.

Feelings tend to follow
thoughts. When we are
aligned, we tend to feel
calm, content, and at
peace with ourselves.

Self - what is in our
heart, soul, and spirit.
We are born whole and
complete in spirit.

SELF

When we are misaligned…

ACTIONS

WORDS

FEELINGS

THOUGHTS

SELF

Actions reveal if we are committed to our true self or to our misaligned beliefs.

Words leak what is going on in our thoughts. They can also be used to redirect our thoughts.

Feelings often match our thoughts. When we are misaligned, we tend to feel negative emotions: fear, guilt, shame, doubt, anxiety, & depression.

Thoughts reflect our beliefs and our beliefs are generally learned from our experiences. Thoughts is where misalignment often starts.

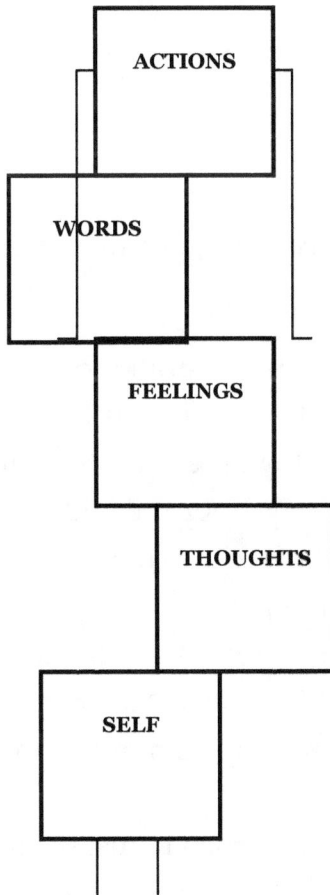

Self - what is in our heart, soul, and spirit. We are born whole and complete in spirit.

3

SELF

"You can never lose your self..."
                    -The Soul

It was a very odd experience, all those years ago when I was ill. The best way to describe it is it seemed like a vision. I was walking to the barn to feed Fifo and was wondering to myself what more I could lose and still be alive. It wasn't an act of feeling sorry for myself; it was more an act of accounting.

I had lost my hair, my looks, my stamina, strength, and independence. I could no longer ride my bike or my horse and had stopped trying. My memory no longer stored information. Due to nerve damage in my hands, my steady penmanship had turned to messy scribble and from nerve damage in my feet, I had to physically look down at my stirrup irons on the rare occasion I did ride my horse to see whether or not my boot had slipped too far into the stirrup. Some friends came around, others stayed away. A whole lot had changed but at the same time, a lot had not changed at all.

While I was walking to the barn, I visualized myself as a large, round ball and every time I identified something that was no longer a part of me or my life, a piece of the ball detached and went away. As one piece after another floated off, the ball became smaller and smaller. Finally what had been a sizeable ball was reduced to a small black dot. That small black dot was what remained of me.

What was this tiny speck, I wondered. Who was I if I was no longer the capable, athletic woman I'd believed myself to be? In my mind's eye, I zoomed in for a closer look at what was left of "me" and the tiny black dot became a key hole. For some reason, I was drawn to look inside the keyhole.

Peering into the dot, I heard a whoosh, and the other side opened up to become a vast, starry, universal sky. It was stunningly silent, peaceful, and beautiful. In that same moment, I heard a voice from deep within me say, "You can never lose yourself."

I'm not sure if I was shocked, awed, or stupefied. Here I was walking through a dusty pasture to feed my horse and I'd just had, what felt to be, a life-altering epiphany. What did it mean? When all the things I'd thought were me dropped away, I was the universe? Could I be making this up or could it be some strange reaction to the chemo drugs?

If it were true, I was not less than I'd thought myself to be, I was more. I was more than I could have imagined: vast, graceful, gently powerful, and as limitless as the universe. If it were true for me, it was true for all of us. In that moment I realized that at our core, all of us are sacred.

So when I began to work on my alignment model, it seemed fitting that the foundation square would be this place, this sacred self. It would be our heart, our spirit, our soul, and our gut. It would include our instincts, intuition, disposition, and personality.

This is the part that each of us is born with, that even when we do not live aligned with it, can never be lost. Because it is perfect already, our self never requires changing; and because it is not based on past, present, or future action, its value is not earned and cannot be deducted. The value of each soul just is.

Yet how can any of us identify something as vast and indescribable as our soul? We are a complex blend of emotions, beliefs, talents, experiences, judgments, expectations, and perceptions. We are taught manners, morals, who we should be, and who we shouldn't. I've heard people say, "I don't know who I am," so how are we to know the truth of who we are and who we aren't?

Fortunately, the soul does speak and we can learn to listen. The soul's voice is a unique voice. It is different than the mindless chatter we often hear as thoughts. Learning to distinguish one voice from another is important. Learning to distinguish the voice of the soul from the voice of mind-chatter is priceless.

SELF

I hear mind-chatter up and around my head. My mind
chatters away, talking quickly, using lots of words,
thinking about this and chatting about that, going on and
on. Once it gets going, the mind chatter almost never
shuts up and is often times negative. It rambles, it
criticizes, it doubts, it rants, it chatters and chatters away.
The soul's voice is a very different voice.

For me, I'm not really sure where the voice of the soul
comes from. I want to say I hear it from deep within, an
origin closer to my heart but at the same time, I might hear
it all around me, as if it's everywhere at once like the
sound of gentle thunder. Regardless of where it comes
from, the soul does not chatter. When I hear it, it speaks
clearly, often slowly, in a deep tone, using few words that
get straight to the point. "You can never lose yourself,"
my soul said to me.

If you want to, you can close your eyes and ask yourself
a question, then wait and listen. The more aware you
become of your soul's voice, the more often you will be
able to hear it.

Here is a simplified example that tends to work for
most people. What is your favorite color? Think of it right
now. If you have several favorite colors, think of each of
them. Whatever color you choose, how do you know
that's your favorite? Are you sure? Notice where your
answers come from. Do you just know?

What if I try to get you to change your mind and make
a different color your favorite? How about orange, doesn't
that sound like a terrific favorite color? It's so bright and

juicy. You could get an orange coat and an orange car. You could buy orange dishes and orange bathroom towels. Does some part in you think that is ridiculous? Do you defend your favorite color?

My favorite color is blue. I have no idea why blue is my favorite color; it just is. Blue has been my favorite color for as long as I can remember. My first bike was blue. Fifo's buckets are blue. Whenever I have a choice between red, yellow, green, or blue, I choose blue. As lovely as orange is in orange juice, it could never be my favorite color. It's just not me.

If we want to, we can begin from who we are and develop more of who we want to become because every person has the seed to every quality already within them. Just like a muscle, we have the ability to develop and condition who we are.

To keep things simple, we can describe ourselves with descriptive words; words like intelligent, capable, good-hearted, loving, creative, or funny. Responsible, playful, strong, sensitive, or resourceful are other descriptive words we might choose. Maybe you are a loving, creative, and capable woman or an honest, honorable, and courageous man.

Some people have a hard time acknowledging themselves. If you have trouble picking three positive words, that's ok. I did, too. When I first did this years ago, the three words that popped out of my mouth were loving, passionate, and committed which seemed ridiculous at the time.

32

Sure, I was loving on the inside but I was a hand-shake person and unbelievably shy. Working so hard just to survive, I felt about as passionate as a rock and the word committed just wasn't reflected by all the unfinished items in my life. The commitments I kept were to other people and the commitments I broke consistently were the ones I made to me. All the same, those were the three words that came to me, so those were my three words.

The surprising thing is that today, I exhibit those qualities. I am loving and now I show it. I am passionate about so many things; animals, people, learning, and sharing that learning with others. I am committed. I am not terribly fast at getting things done but I rarely give up. Those three qualities, I have developed in me.

We can realign ourselves so that our actions and belief systems do match who we are. It's not who we are that is deficient – it's who we think we are, who we feel we are, who we say we are, and who we act like we are that may need a change.

Acknowledging the positive truth about ourselves may not be easy for several reasons. While growing up, we may have been told that when we make mistakes, we are no longer good. We may have been told that if we got an answer wrong that we are stupid, or that if we ever told a lie, we are no longer an honest person.

Additionally, we may have been taught that if we acknowledge the positive truth about ourselves, we are self-centered, conceited, or egotistical. Most people are taught not to be a show-off and not to brag. In reality, when we value ourselves appropriately we can, in turn, value others appropriately. To be truly, "self-centered" is to be centered with our self and being centered with our self is a good thing.

If a person is talented, charismatic, and creative it's not a matter of bragging to acknowledge the talent, charisma, and creativity. It is simply a matter of being accurate; yet many people have a difficult time representing their qualities accurately. We may have a hard time accepting compliments. Instead of saying "Thank you," and acknowledging our talents, we might say something dismissing like, "You're too kind."

It's as if we're trying to convince everyone, we're less than who we are rather than simply being who we are. Imagine if a person had black hair but was told it was bragging to call it black. Since the person didn't want to brag, imagine if they told everyone their hair was green because green seemed more socially acceptable. Would their hair be green? Of course not because black hair is black regardless of what a person calls it.

What if that person actually dyed their hair green so it appeared green? Other people would see it as green and they would call it green, too, but would the true hair color be green? Of course not. Black hair is black and no matter what name you call it or what color you dye it, it will always be the true color at its roots. Our roots are our true color, too.

Being accurate is not about being conceited nor humble. Being accurate has everything to do with being real. A

battery has power whether it is activated or not. A
Porsche has power whether it is driven fast or kept parked
in a garage. So do we. Whether we acknowledge the truth
of who we are, or we deny the truth of who we are, it does
not change the truth.

To acknowledge the positive truths about yourself, all
the evidence you need has already taken place in your life
if you will simply take a moment to find it. If you've ever
done a courageous thing even one time in your whole life;
you have the quality of courage within you. If you've ever
been compassionate even once, it is proof that compassion
is in your ability because if that quality was not within
you, you could not have acted on the quality. It's that
simple.

As people, we are sort of funny. We misunderstand
things a lot. If we're walking along, we tend to easily
acknowledge that we can walk because we have the
evidence that we are walking. If we suddenly trip and fall,
we may think to ourselves, "I can't even walk. All I can do
is trip!" That sort of statement, however, is not true.
Walking is walking and tripping is tripping. Tripping and
walking are not the same. One action does not take away
the validity of the other action. We can do both.

In life, some of us tend to look at the times we've
tripped as evidence that we cannot walk. I don't know
about you, but I can do something rather brilliant one day
and something rather idiotic the next. One quality does
not negate the opposite quality yet I've heard myself say
to myself, "I can't get anything right." Sure I can get

things right and I can also get things wrong. So can everybody.

We live in a world of complimentary opposites; friendly, shy, fast, slow, warm, cold. We have the ability to act on opposing qualities at any given time, sometimes at nearly the same time, and the existence of one quality does not negate the other.

If you have ever demonstrated kindness, that is proof that kindness is within your ability. So is it within your ability to demonstrate the opposite trait of unkindness. The question is, who are you really, deep down inside? If you happen to act unkindly, is that who you truly are, or might that be an example when your words or actions did not match yourself? Only you can decide. The choice is always, and only, our own choice.

Once an action is in the past, however, the personal trait required to take that action is proven and can be safely stored for all time. No matter how much our misaligned belief systems may try to convince us to the contrary, past evidence of our abilities cannot ever be removed once it's been proven.

Please take a moment to do the following exercise. Choose a positive quality in yourself even if you don't currently believe it. For the sake of this exercise, I will make up an example person. Let's say this person is a successful, intelligent individual who has felt like a failure. As I take you through this example, you can choose your own word and do the exercise for yourself.

So here is how the exercise works. Pick a quality that you would like to be or become more of. I'll use the word, capable. Take your age and look over the last ten years. Find evidence within your life of the word you choose. The evidence is there, if you look for it. I promise.

If you're mind tries to give you examples of times you were the opposite of that trait, please skip over those examples for now. Those are examples of tripping and even though I am sure you have tripped with the best, right now I am asking you to find evidence of walking not tripping.

Our example person is thirty-five years old. They have had a relatively 'normal' life, yet inside they feel like a failure. Are they a failure or are they capable? Let's see?

Between thirty-five and twenty-five, where have they shown themselves as capable? When they were 34, they bought a house and had their eighth wedding anniversary. During those years, they became a parent and got a job.

Ten years before that would be fifteen to twenty-five. They successfully completed high school, successfully completed college, and got married. Are you seeing how this works?

Finally, we'll look at their life from five to fifteen. They won a medal swimming, completed grammar school, and took care of a lost dog until the owners could be found.

What do you think; is this person a failure or does their life lend substantial evidence of their value? Are they capable or incapable? Maybe a more accurate way to represent themselves instead of, "I am a failure," would be, "I am valuable."

Think of a quality and look back over the last ten years of your own life. Notice all of the times when that quality showed up. If you take the time to really look, you will find example after example after example. You may remember important things that you've forgotten.

When I did this exercise, I was searching for the word committed as I felt I was having trouble being committed to finishing things that I wanted to complete. I was sure I was uncommitted.

After going back in time, I remembered something I had completely forgotten; when I was twenty, I saved a man from drowning and although there were two other people on the shore, I was the one who was committed enough to jump in the water and help him. Here I helped save a man's life and my memory didn't even bother to recall it! You will be amazed at what you will remember, too.

Every quality is already a part of you. You can think, speak, and act in alignment with who you are already and you can strengthen who you want to become. When I was first learning to do this, a friend of mine suggested an idea to me. She said, "Ask yourself a simple question, 'Who are you, Faith? Are you this quality or are you the opposite quality?' Then choose."

It wasn't long after, that I had an emergency with my dog. In attempting to eat peanut butter out of a plastic jar, Rufus ingested some of the lid which was on the verge of perforating his intestine. Until he had stayed at the vet clinic overnight and tests were run, we didn't know what had caused his problem. The tests and stabilization were already over a thousand dollars when the vet phoned and said that they needed to do surgery immediately or he would die.

My mind raced with the expense. My dog was twelve. The vet couldn't be certain that even with the surgery he would make it but the vet did say she thought he probably would. I asked for twenty minutes to drive to the clinic and see my dog. While I was driving, I kept hearing my friend's question going through my mind, "Who are you, Faith?"

Just that morning in writing an email to a friend, I wrote that I was a person who does not give up easily. Suddenly, I knew the question to ask myself. "Are you a person who doesn't give up easily or are you a person who quits?" I knew then exactly what I must do.

When I got to the clinic, I asked the vet to try to save my dog. I realized that no matter the outcome, I had done the right thing for me because I had stayed true to myself in not giving up. I would know that I had tried. I have never regretted times in my life when I have tried. I have only regretted the times I haven't.

Rufus lived through the surgery to remain a part of my life to the ripe old age of fifteen. The bill came out to be exquisitely expensive. It took a long time to pay off the money but it wasn't too bad when I thought of what the cost would be prorated and spread across fifteen years of having such a wonderful dog.

Not long after the surgery, I remembered a time when Rufus was younger and a friend and I got ourselves stranded overnight on the side of a mountain while hiking. Once darkness fell, there was no choice but to sit down and wait for morning. Just before we stopped, we saw a bear and the terrain we were in is known for mountain lions.

All night, Rufus and my other dog, Sam, guarded the two of us while we shivered in our t-shirts and shorts. The dogs took turns rushing at the nearby bushes and by morning, both dog's feet were torn and ripped from spending all night running on shale.

I'm sure Rufus did not consider what it might cost him to protect us that night. Had the bear come back, Rufus would not have sat there and had a conversation about what he should or shouldn't do. Looking back, I wish I could show as much loyalty in all of my decisions as my dogs have always instinctively and immediately shown toward me.

None of us is perfect, yet on the soul level we are each perfect in our otherwise imperfection. We can choose to relate to one another beyond all of our mistakes and blunders. We can choose to see the best in each other and ourselves, and do our best to overlook the rest. Truly, each one of us is sacred so when we see one another as the best of who we are, the soul may feel comfortable enough to venture outward and be known. Some cultures actually view the soul as being on the outside of a person rather than on the inside.

For alignment, the self is the foundation block and it provides the compass for our lives. It tells us how we are doing and when we need a course correction. With practice, we can learn to hear our soul's voice and distinguish it from the other forms of self-talk in our mind.

In subsequent chapters, we will learn to use our self as a guide against which to align the other blocks, but first we will review each block individually. The next block is thoughts.

4

THOUGHTS / BELIEFS

"Whether you think you can or you think you can't, you're right."
-Henry Ford

During my recovery I read a book called, "You Can't Afford The Luxury of a Negative Thought." It was written by a man who was HIV positive and was one of the most life-changing books I've ever read. The revelation for me was to learn just how important these invisible little things that float between our ears are. The thoughts we think and emotions we subsequently feel, connect with our nervous systems and immune systems to affect our physical bodies and our health.

I remember reading about a person who had multiple personality disorder. One personality was allergic to orange juice and would break out in hives while the other personality could drink orange juice without incident. The

42

idea that thoughts could have such a drastic and immediate effect seemed crazy, but the more I've come to learn about thoughts, the more important they seem to be.

It's in our thoughts where alignment or misalignment almost always starts. If our thoughts match our self, we are in alignment. If our thoughts do not match our self, we are out of alignment and all our other parts get misaligned from there.

Misaligned beliefs comes from multiple sources and can happen early. From birth, we are deluged with information. Our parents, teachers, television, and the media are full of messages. We're taught what is good and what is bad; what is right and what is wrong according to the source it is coming from. In an effort to be good parents, parents generally teach their children similar beliefs that were taught to them. The ham story is a good example.

At Thanksgiving, a young girl notices that her mother chops the ends off the ham before placing it in the oven. When she asks her mother why she does so, the mother thinks about it for a moment and says that Grandma taught her to do it that way.

Since Grandma is in the living room, the child asks Grandma why she chops the ends off the ham. Grandma thinks about it for a moment and shares that she's not really sure except that Great Grandma did it that way.

Well, Great Grandma is also at the house for Thanksgiving dinner so when the child asks Great Grandma, Great Grandma shares that she always chopped the ends off the ham because she couldn't afford to buy a pan large enough for the ham to fit in whole.

When we do things without knowing why we do them, or believe something from some inner expectation that we 'should' believe it, it may be that we simply got taught something by somebody who got taught the same thing by somebody else and so on. Unlike the ham story, we don't always get to find out where we learned it or why.

Children are like little sponges absorbing information. As children, we are inclined to accept whatever opinions are offered because we don't develop the ability to evaluate circumstances on our own until later in our lives.

Additionally, children tend to be ego-centric which means, we tend to believe that everything in the world revolves around us or is caused by us. Consider how common it is that children from divorced families are inclined to think the divorce was their fault. Consider how common it is that children who have received abuse are inclined to think they did something to cause it.

I remember an incident from my own childhood. I was probably seven years old. Some of my extended family members had come for dinner and I had taken them outside to watch me do a death drop from the jungle gym bars in the back yard.

Swinging from the bars was something I practiced often at school and I was amongst the best of my friends at being able to do difficult routines. So, with my aunt and uncle watching, from the high bar I swung backward with no hands, flipped myself forward from my knees, let go of the bar and landed squarely on both feet. Taa-daa! I'd done a death drop!

Just then, my aunt burst out laughing. "I saw your underwear! Ha-ha! Ha-ha! Ha-ha!" She ran in the house to let everyone know that Faith had swung from the bars wearing a skirt and she could see my underwear. I felt humiliated and for the first time in my life, I felt self-conscious about my body.

Intense experiences lead to intense memories and intense memories often lead to deeply embedded internalized beliefs. The first time we encounter a new experience, our memories 'learn.'

Weak experiences, like what we ate for breakfast, create short term memories that are soon forgotten. Strong experiences, like "Oh my God! What have you done?!" or "Yow! I just burned my forehead with the curling iron!!!" actually cause our memory cells to change. This may be why beliefs formed from traumatic events can be so hard to get over. If we are making a mountain out of a molehill, it could be that the mountain is made because of a chemical change in our memory cells.

Cellular memories formed from painful experiences, like don't put your hand on a hot stove, are intended to last a lifetime in order to protect us from being hurt; but self-critical beliefs we generate about ourselves actually tend to induce our being hurt as we build walls that prevent us from receiving the very things we desire and need.

Instead of rejecting false beliefs as false, it's like we build a little house for them inside our heads so the wrong beliefs can move in and become a part of us! False beliefs mix with true beliefs, contradict each other, and cause confusion. "Who am I?" becomes a good question. Fortunately, beliefs can be changed and we can make new beliefs to counteract old ones. We can use our thoughts like a reset button. We can reject wrong beliefs.

Some people call these false beliefs, "the critic," yet as one false belief builds on top of another false belief, it may feel that you have more than one critic and may have generated an entire committee. Wouldn't it be nice if instead of negative beliefs, we had the Dallas cowboy cheerleaders in our minds cheering us on with only positive beliefs?

Many of us end up creating very similar wrong beliefs. "I am not good enough." "I am not lovable." "I am stupid." "I don't deserve anything good." "I'm not attractive." "No one could love me if they really knew me." "I am a failure." These false core beliefs seem to affect every single person at one time or another and are often the cause when behavior is erratic or doesn't make sense.

Living on his own at ninety-five, still energetic and spry, my grandpa seems to know a thing or two about life. He says, "Don't build fences. Don't put up blocks and tell yourself you can't do things because of this reason or that. Don't lock yourself into a certain amount of time because if you don't achieve what you want by the time you think you should have, you may get discouraged and quit. Just keep at it. When you hit an obstacle, put your brain in gear and start thinking."

When something goes wrong, how often do you hear yourself say, "I'm smart. I can handle this." "I'm loveable. I'll get through this." "I deserve good things. I won't take this personally." "Set backs are normal. I'll just keep going." The problem is that misaligned beliefs are false but they often feel real.

Because we filter our environment, we may only notice those things that cause the negative beliefs to appear true and overlook everything else. The last time you lost your car keys, did you say to yourself, "Boy, I haven't lost my keys in ages. I am so organized." Yet don't we find our keys more often than we lose them?

We literally receive only a portion of the information available to us because our brain has a filter that lets in what we are looking for and filters out the rest. Take a moment and try this. Just real quick, look around you and notice everything you can that is white.

Ok. Did you do it? Now, close your eyes and list off everything you can remember that was white. Great. How many did you get? Feel free to look around and notice all the white that you remembered.

Now, without looking, close your eyes and list as many things as you possibly can that were black. Black?!?! Yes, now keep your eyes on the page and do not look. Close your eyes and remember everything you can. Do it now.

Ok, well done. Now go ahead and look around to purposely notice the black. Was it easier to notice the white you were looking for than the black that you weren't looking for? Notice how much green is around you, how much red, and how much blue. When you were looking for white, your eyes saw everything. How much of everything did you notice or did you mostly notice what you were looking for?

When a person is confident, they will likely hear the sentence, "You look lovely today," as a compliment meaning, you look lovely today. When a person is unconfident, they may filter that same statement and instead hear, "You look nice today but you look lousy most days," or they may not hear the compliment at all and wonder why no one ever says anything nice to them.

The name of this filter in our brain is the Reticular Activation System and it filters information based on our past experiences, habits, and conditioning. With awareness, we can reprogram it!

Because we tend to make decisions according to our beliefs, it is very important to be aware of what the beliefs are. A man once told me he realized he'd been causing problems in his relationship because on some level, he believed that being in a good relationship was too good to be true. His parents had divorced and he absorbed an idea that good relationships can't last.

So, when things were going well, he almost couldn't help but make a problem. Once he generated conflict, he could be right that good relationships can't last and things

48

had been too good to be true. At some point, this man came to his own awareness and stopped sabotaging himself. Once he changed his beliefs, his relationships got better, and he felt happier.

All the beliefs we hold about ourselves, we made up in the first place and we can make up new, more accurate beliefs any time. One way to change beliefs is to reject false beliefs as false. Like the saying goes, if the shoe fits wear it but if the shoe doesn't fit, don't put it on and certainly don't try to run a life-long race in the wrong shoes.

Imagine trading shoes with someone two sizes smaller than you. The other person's shoes are so nice. They are the highest grade Italian leather and work brilliantly for the other person. They seem so nice that even though they don't fit you, you put them on. What happens as you try to walk? What happens as you try to run?

Imagine going back to the shoe owner and explaining your problem. "Hi. I'm really sorry but I'm having a hard time walking in these shoes because I think they are too small for me. I need to take them off."

Imagine the shoe owner responds with, "Well, I don't know what to tell you. Those shoes are the best around. There is nothing wrong with them; they work great for me. The fact that you are now crippled must be a reflection of your inadequacy. There is nothing wrong with the shoes so there must be something wrong with you." People tend to offer beliefs that work well for them but that doesn't mean that their beliefs will work well for others. It's ok to keep beliefs that fit and reject the ones that don't.

Some people believe that our negative beliefs are tied to our survival instinct in that the beliefs persuade us not to deviate from our norm. "You can't do that. You are going to fail. Don't try anything new. Stay here with what you already know, like procrastination, dirty dishes, and unpaid bills. Don't do anything different. Something really terrible could happen if we don't know what to expect." But here is a thought; what if the negative voice in our head is actually our friend and not our foe?

I was thinking one day about my own little voice that rattles around in my own head. Why would I have such a nasty, destructive, mean, and evil part of myself? Why do all of us have one? It just didn't feel right and it didn't make sense.

Our bodies are made to do everything they can to heal. If we get a germ, our white cells do their best to fight it. If we break a bone, our body goes about healing it and if the bone isn't set straight, our bodies will even heal the bone crooked. So, if my entire body is geared toward health and healing as best it can, why wouldn't my mind be geared toward healing, too? Then I got it. Perhaps it is!

I started thinking carefully about my little voice and I noticed that it only comes up in specific areas of my life. It never bothers me about running for congress or changing the oil in my car myself because I don't care about achieving those things. My voice doesn't bother me when

I get on a plane to fly somewhere and it doesn't tell me that I should own my own airline or fly my own plane.

My voice does bother me, however, about things I do care about. It bothers me about balancing my check book and keeping my house in order. It bothers me about staying in shape and taking good care of myself. I have not always been as strong in these areas as I want to be and my nasty little voice is a pointer-outer, a challenger, of where I want to get stronger and where I need to grow.

All of the sudden, I saw my little voice differently. I pictured it poking me in my chest, enticing me to fight it. "What are you going to do about it, huh? Are you going to prove me wrong for once in your life and go for a run or are you going to let me be right while you go back to bed?" or "Are you going to worry yourself silly over what other people might think or are you going to realize that most people aren't even thinking about you because maybe they're busy thinking about what everybody else is thinking!"

Wow…everything it said to me, might just mean the opposite. If my voice says black, probably it's white. When my little voice tells me I can't, what if that means I can?

What I suddenly realized is when I have gotten strong enough to prove the voice wrong consistently in any particular area, like washing the dishes in my sink, the voice shuts up and leaves me alone about that particular thing. The voice finds another area that I need to get stronger in, and it starts bothering me there. No matter how strong I get, the voice finds one new place after another and helps me to get stronger. Getting me stronger seems to be its job.

One day I was thinking about all the things I wanted to get done when I heard my little voice pipe in, "You'll never get all of that done." Then I translated my little voice to mean the opposite. If it says I can't get my list done, then it must mean that I can.

"Of course you can," I heard another part of myself say. Maybe I wouldn't get everything done that day but if I didn't stop, of course I would get each thing done. I am a strong, capable, and resourceful woman. It suddenly seemed so simple.

Here is what I now know about my little voice which I suspect is true of everyone's little voice. If the voice uses shame, blame, fear, guilt, or self-doubt, that is a tip off that the message is coming from a false belief and is meant to mean the opposite. Shame, blame, fear, guilt, and self-doubt are immediate indicators that we are misaligned because our soul has nothing to feel shame, blame, fear, guilt, or doubt for.

People often feel guilty when they make mistakes but part of who we are is that we do make mistakes. We are human. Getting things wrong is how we learn. The important thing is to keep learning.

I shared my theory with a friend. A few weeks later, I got an excited phone call from him. "I was in Florida and I used your theory. You are right! It totally worked!"

My friend explained that he had been on a group tour of a swamp and that he'd had a wonderful time. When the tour was over, he wanted to rent a small boat and go exploring on his own. My friend loves swamps. Then he heard the little voice in his head telling him not to go, that it could be dangerous because the swamp was filled with alligators.

"You didn't go, did you?" I was alarmed. "I didn't mean that you should go into alligator-infested waters!"

"I did go! I had the best time. I am so glad you told me about translating the voice to mean the opposite because I probably wouldn't have gone for it. I explored the swamp for hours on my own, turning down all these nooks and crannies. I even brought some swamp water home in a bottle so you can smell it. It is the most amazing water ever. Thank you so much! I never would have done that had it not been for you!"

I thought a lot about my friend's story and also about safety. What if doing the opposite wasn't such a great idea, but then I realized something surprising. When I have truly been in a dangerous situation, I don't sit around and have a conversation with myself. When I am truly in danger, I act and act fast.

"Faith, the horse is running straight at you. Maybe you should move out of the way!"

"Nah...I'll just stand here and see what happens." I don't think so.

The survival instinct is very different from the negative little voice. One is all talk and the other is all action. The point I am trying to make is that if we don't correct our limiting beliefs, we are likely to act limited. Not only would that rip us off from the fullness of our own lives, but if we live as less than who we are, we would also rip off other people who might benefit from our wholeness.

How tragic would it be if Mark Twain believed he was too stupid to write so he never wrote a story, or if John Lennon believed he was too bad to sing so he never sang a song? If you believe you don't deserve to be happy so you don't give yourself the chance to live the best life possible, then other people pay the price with you for your false beliefs.

If you know a person whose behavior doesn't make sense to you, remember how strong false beliefs can be and how easily all of us form them. That person's actions may be stemming from beliefs that cause them to think they "aren't good enough" to do something different. They may have had a strong life event that formed a belief that something is "too good to be true" so they find a way to wreck it. Then they can be right about the wrong belief. "See, it's wrecked. I knew it was too good to be true!"

When we self-sabotage, we generally do so in order to align with the false beliefs rather than aligning with our true self but remember, our beliefs can change. The more we relate to one another from the best of who we are or might be, the more self-esteem we each gain. As we form more and more supportive beliefs, the more our feelings, words, and actions will begin to reflect them.

THOUGHTS/BELIEFS

We can choose what we will or will not believe about ourselves and we can choose what we will or will not believe about others. We can choose empowering beliefs that we are worthy, kind, deserving, good enough, fun, intelligent, and human. We can choose to see others as their best and not their worst. We can choose alignment.

The more we translate the negative voice, do the opposite, and align with the soul, the easier it will become to act in alignment. When our thoughts change, our feelings change. That leads us to the next block in our alignment process. The next block is feelings.

5

FEELINGS

Emotions are like the wind...they come and go....the good, the bad, and the ugly...you just have to see them as not permanent."
— Martin Murphy

"You want to put a coring needle the size of an ice pick where?"

In the early stages of diagnosis, the doctors needed a tissue sample to figure out if the mass in my chest was malignant or benign. The procedure would require pushing a coring needle, which looked like an ice pick, through my chest wall and between my ribs which would hopefully land in the tumor without puncturing my lung. Puncturing my lung was a 30% probability.

"If my lung gets punctured, how will I breath?" The thought of a punctured lung terrified me.

56

"We would just keep you hospitalized for a few days until it healed."

"No, no..." I thought to myself. "That doesn't sound good. I like my lungs just fine the way they are. There's got to be another way." There was.

The alternative was knocking me out, cutting a small incision at the base of my throat, putting the needle beneath my ribcage, and getting a tissue sample while I was sleeping. Perfect! I'll be sleeping and the doctors can do whatever they'd like. My mother thought otherwise.

"If you go that route, you will have a scar on your neck for the rest of your life," she said.

"So what," I thought. "I'll be sleeping."

My mother was persistent. "You've got to think about the future. You're going to live a long time. Trust me, you don't want a scar on your neck for the rest of your life."

The truth was, I was afraid and I wanted to get away from the fear. Everything was happening so fast. Not more than a week earlier, I'd been having simple chest pains but overall I was fine and now, one week later, I was facing a probable cancer diagnosis and all of the diagnostic tests and procedures that went along with it.

With the help of valium, I let them push the coring needle through my chest and closed my eyes to avoid seeing the handle sticking out of me while they took a ct scan to be sure the end of the needle had reached the tumor. One sample wasn't enough. In order to be sure, they wanted two so I closed my eyes and we did it again.

I felt the same fear almost every time there was a new test to take or a new piece of information to learn. I had a bone marrow biopsy which involved lying face down on a table while the doctor shoved a sharp instrument all the way to the inside of my hip bone. There is no way to numb the inside of the bone which is lined with nerve endings so rather than a traditional pain killer, the doctor gave me mind-altering drugs to help disassociate me from my body.

There was a nuclear scan which involved injecting radioactive dye into my lymph nodes so the nodes would show up on an x-ray. The books I read said that the red colored Adriamycin drug I'd be taking might turn my pee red. One of the other drugs I would receive was Nitrogen Mustard, the same drug used in agent orange during Vietnam.

There were many times my feelings screamed, no, while my mind and often times my mother, guided me carefully and steadily forward to yes. Yes, I would take these tests. Yes, I would take the chemo drugs. Yes, I would take the radiation. Yes, I would do whatever I was told to do in order to have the best chance at living. Fortunately, it worked.

I could not allow myself to make decisions based solely on my feelings. My feelings told me to jump up and run out of the room while the tumor in my chest, which had already grown so large as to smash one lung, bump into my heart, and start spreading my ribcage, would have grown even larger and eventually killed me. With all due respect to my feelings, my feelings didn't matter. The only thing that mattered was the end result that I live.

It seems like I'd been taught to hold feelings as all important but had I based my decisions solely from them, my decisions would have been based from the feeling of fear. Actually, I would have been making decisions to avoid fear, but sometimes fear can't be avoided. Sometimes we get to feel the fear and do what we must do anyway. All I really wanted was to be happy.

How many times have you heard someone say, "I just want to be happy." Isn't that what everyone wants? We want to feel good. Isn't it because of our feelings that we buy the nicer car and the bigger house? Don't we want the chocolate bar or the new puppy because we want to feel good?

Ask anyone why they want whatever they want and once you get down to the root cause you will find that people simply want to feel good emotionally. Even when people alter their state with drugs or alcohol, they are generally trying to make themselves feel better with the substance than they think they feel without it. But when the new car gets old, the chocolate is gone, or the new puppy pees on the rug, how do we feel then? The trouble seems to be that the good feelings never last but on the flip side, neither do the bad ones.

So how do feelings work and why do they tend to be so transitory and fleeting? Aren't we supposed to trust our feelings? What most people don't realize is that feelings are designed to change constantly. Like a thermostat set to register an alarm bell or an all's clear, it's the job of our feelings to constantly give us signals based on our interpretation of events. Think of feelings like a flashing red at an intersection. They don't say when to go, when to stop, or what to do. They do say, "Hey, pay attention here. There is something you need to be aware of."

Feelings have a real job. They give us life or death signals for our safety. They also let us know if we are in alignment with ourselves or if there is a change we need to make. When we are aligned, the feelings that result tend to include peace, gratitude, joy, compassion, and contentment. When we are out of alignment, feelings like stress, shame, guilt, self-doubt, blame, and fear show up.

Emotional reactions are built in to protect us from danger, to let us know if our needs are being met, and to point out some sort of change we might need to make. However, the key distinction is that our feelings change as our interpretations change, so feelings are closely linked to our thoughts. Studies have shown that our mind does not know the difference between what is true and what we believe to be true. Our mind will believe whatever we tell it whether or not it is accurate, and our feelings will respond accordingly. Here is an example.

Imagine someone in your life who is precious and important to you. Maybe it's your child, spouse, or close friend. Imagine they are on their way to your house but they are late and this person generally keeps their word and is on time. You heard sirens a while back and didn't think much of it but as the time ticks on, you're beginning to wonder what has happened and you begin to feel a bit concerned. Where are they, you wonder. Why haven't they called?

Suddenly, there is a knock at the door and a very somber policeman says he has some bad news for you; there's been a serious accident. Just for a moment, allow this example to be real for you and notice how you're feeling. Is there a tightening in your stomach or a shortness to your breath? What are you feeling? Just notice. What thoughts are going through your mind?

All of a sudden, the policeman looks at your house address and says, "Isn't this 1482 Maple Street? I'm sorry. I'm at the wrong house. I've got to go." As suddenly as he arrived, the policeman is gone. Just then the phone rings.

It's the voice of that special person you've been waiting for. "I'm sorry I'm so late. There was a terrible accident and my cell battery died. I had to find a pay phone just to call you. I'm almost there."

How are you feeling now? Are you feeling any differently than you were a few moments ago? If you are, what changed? Did the truth change or did what you thought was true change? Feelings do not know what is real from what is imagined. They are reactions to our thoughts and they believe whatever our thoughts tell them is true.

If you responded like most people, you felt the possibility that your loved one might be dead and then relief that they were alive. Your feelings likely followed the information that was given. Feelings are not wrong or right. Feelings just are.

When I thought my lung might collapse from the coring needle biopsy, I felt afraid. When I learned that a collapsed lung was not fatal, I felt less afraid. Once the procedure was over and I learned that my lung had not collapsed, I felt relieved.

When we interpret information accurately, feelings can help us with when to go, when to stop, and when to proceed with caution, but if we interpret information incorrectly and then act on that misinterpretation, feelings can set us up for a train wreck. Some of the worst, most impulsive decisions ever made are decisions that stem from strong emotions which tend to cause people to act quickly and emotionally, without thinking.

Imagine seeing your significant other standing beside a very attractive person of the opposite sex. Your loved one hasn't seen you yet and suddenly he or she reaches over and gives that other person a very close and intimate hug. You approach. How are you feeling? Your loved one is smiling hugely at the other person and can't seem to take his or her eyes off of them. Is there anything you might like to do or say when you get there? They hug the other person a second time right in front of you!

Finally your loved one sees you, rushes over happily and says, "Honey, I'm so glad to see you! This is cousin so and so from Idaho. I'm so glad you're here. Great Aunt Betty is in town, too. I can't wait for you to meet her!"

What thoughts were going through your mind as you approached and what if you had acted on those thoughts without questioning them? Might this story have had a different ending? Our feelings are important yet when we make decisions based on feelings alone, we are prone to being reactive, impulsive, and act in ways that we may regret later.

When people act in emotionally erratic ways, it is often a sign of a core fear belief triggering. "I am not good enough." "I am not lovable." "I am stupid." "I don't deserve anything good." "I'm not attractive." "No one could love me if they really knew me." "All I do is fail."

If you are experiencing erratic behavior in yourself or someone else, keep in mind that everyone has core fear beliefs that sometimes trigger. Sometimes we need reassurance. Sometimes we need encouragement. Sometimes we need a reminder that our core fear beliefs are just beliefs.

Feelings come before an event in anticipation but they also come after an event, too. Most of us tend to put more weight on the feelings we have before taking action yet how good are our decisions when we base them on what we feel, or don't feel, like doing?

"I think I'll go exercise. Nah, I don't feel like it." "I think I'll get started on my homework. Nah, I'll go get a snack instead." "Look, a new car. It feels so nice during this test drive. I'll sign up for the credit option so I can take it home today!"

Do you feel better before you exercise or after? Do you feel better before you pay the bills or after? Do you feel better before you clean the house or after?

Many of us have been taught to trust our feelings and base important decisions from them, but feelings are different than instinct and intuition. Intuition and instinct come from the foundation of self and can be trusted. Feelings that come as a reaction to events often change by the hour and sometimes by the minute. In stock trading, it's a common rule that emotions are the enemy because emotions can cause a person to make hasty decisions based on fear or greed.

Our feelings can be so erratic, up, down, over, up. Keeping our feelings in a positive state can be challenging and is not always possible because life is ever changing and feelings are designed to change in response to life. My wise Aunt Barbara once said that keeping a steady state can be like trying to rake leaves into a pile in the middle of a wind storm. For all the leaves that stay in the pile, the wind comes along sweeping a lot of them back out. With practice, however, we can improve our ability to manage our emotional state by checking our interpretations and noticing if our thoughts, words, and actions are congruent with what is in our heart.

In his ground-breaking work, John Castagnini explains how we become emotionally charged. Because all things are made up of atoms, and all atoms have both protons and electrons, all things have both a positive and negative charge to them at all times.

FEELINGS

When we are experiencing a negative emotion, we are noticing only the negative aspects of something and we are failing to notice the positive aspects that are also there. When we are experiencing a positive emotion, we are noticing only the positive aspects of something and we are not noticing what is negative about it. All things have both positive and negative aspects at all times so if we can notice what is positive and also what is negative, we will equilibrate the emotional charge and return to a more neutral state. It may sound technical and complicated at first but in truth, it's pretty simple.

In eighth grade, I had a sweet boyfriend I'll call Jay. When we got to high school, a lot of new boys suddenly showed interest. Jay didn't show a whole lot of interest in me so I broke up with him to go out with the new boys. Surprisingly to me, Jay was suddenly heart-broken. I hadn't thought from his actions that he liked me all that much and I also hadn't thought to ask.

It didn't take long before I realized that the new boys were not better than Jay and I wanted Jay back. Jay wouldn't take me back; not as a Freshman, a Sophomore, or ever. Now I was the one who was heart-broken. What could possibly be good about that?

What was good about that was it was an important lesson early on for me in not taking people for granted. I've been mindful ever since to take the best care of my relationships that I can, and to not assume the grass is greener somewhere else. The opposite can be done for things that we are positively charged about.

Have you ever fallen in love? Do you remember how perfect that person seemed to be in those first few days or weeks? We notice everything that we love about the other person, and there are plenty of positive things to love, but if we are only noticing the positive aspects, we are forgetting to notice what we don't like so much about that person. Instead of recognizing them as a whole person with both strengths and flaws, we tend to put them on an unrealistic pedestal from which they eventually fall.

In time, the same person that seemed so terrific can later seem awful. Why? Because sometimes, we switch over to noticing only the negative aspects of the person and omit the positive aspects that we used to see. They snore, squeeze the tooth paste wrong, show up late, or do something else that bugs us. We forget about all the things we used to adore about them that are likely still there. Now we are unbalanced in the opposite direction.

What works better in keeping our emotions balanced is to notice the positive and negative in all things so that there is balance to both sides. Positive and negative are merely our own judgment anyway, yet seeing two sides to things can cause us to feel much more centered and stable emotionally. Steady feelings can act like lubricant and cause our gears to run smoothly while unsteady feelings can feel like sand in the gears and make movement and action feel overwhelmingly difficult.

Another way to manage emotions, feel better, and gain confidence is to anchor our emotions firmly to the foundation of our self. If who we are is an intelligent, capable, and resourceful person then when the boss changes the computer system, we don't need to become reactive or to get upset. We can remember who we are and know that since we are intelligent, capable, and resourceful, we can learn the new system.

It may feel like happiness is out there somewhere outside of ourselves. If we have a better car, a better spouse, or if we please people, then we can feel good. Have you noticed that once people get what they want, the good feelings soon wear off and it's not long until they want something different? Generally, what we want is the next thing that we don't yet have.

Trying to make ourselves feel good with external validation happens when we try to fill ourselves from the outside with things like cars, clothes, or other people's opinions. The good feelings don't last because we are not made to fill ourselves up. We are made to empty ourselves out. Joy comes not from trying to fill our emptiness but from sharing our fullness. Love, joy, caring, compassion; these qualities radiate out, not in.

Have you ever wanted someone to love you knowing that if you could just be loved, it would fill you up inside? And have you ever been loved or admired by someone you didn't particularly like? If so, how did it feel to be loved by someone you didn't love back? Did their love fill you up inside or did it make you want to cringe? Being loved is not the same as being loving.

When we love and are loving, we experience the sensation of love. Love is a glow that extends outward.

It's nicest to love and be loved in return, yet we can even feel love for inanimate objects like our car, our home, or our professions. We tend to feel joy in our experience of loving whatever it is that we love.

Joy, gratitude, and love emerge from within us much like a work of art that lies within the artist waiting to be created. Once the paint goes on the canvas, what was on the inside of the artist is now visible on the outside to be given as a gift to the world. We, too, are a gift to the world and we tend to feel the most joy when our inside shows on our outside.

Self, thoughts, and feelings are on the inside of a person and because they are on the inside they can be a little tricky to manage. Words and actions, however, are on the outside of a person and can be consciously directed.

To recondition our thoughts, train our feelings, and prepare to take action, we can learn to consciously use our words. The next block in the alignment process is words.

6

WORDS

"Words are like the God, Janus, they face outwards and inwards at once." John O'Donohue

"There is no way I'm gaining fifty pounds. I'm sorry but that is not an option."

The one positive thing that went through my mind when I got the cancer diagnosis was a shallow thing but the truth is, I thought to myself, "Finally, I am going to get to be one of those skinny people like I've seen on t.v."

So when the doctor told me I'd be taking high doses of prednisone which would cause me to gain fifty pounds, that didn't fit with my vision of what a cancer patient looks like. Weight loss was the one and only positive thing I could think of, and I was not going to let that go.

"Fine, I won't eat," I told the doctor.

"It doesn't matter," he responded. "Prednisone will make you ravenously hungry and if you don't eat, your face will get puffed up and you will get what we call 'moon face.' That's just the way it is."

"Nope. That's not happening to me."

Weight loss has never been an easy thing for me. I had spent the last several months running, biking, and sweating my last ten pounds off. I'm the kind of person who can gain weight simply by looking at food and I was finally in the best shape of my adult life. I had to deal with all the tests, the bald head, and all the other symptoms, but gaining fifty pounds, being bald and fat, that was something I just couldn't handle.

As the days went on, not only did I not gain weight but I lost an additional twelve pounds from my already trim frame. The bone structure in my face became refined and my hip bones stuck out to the point that wearing a seat belt in the car was pleasantly uncomfortable. I got what I'd wanted. I looked like the people I'd seen on t.v.

The only thing I can account this to was my unyielding resolve that my body would not have the typical reaction to the prednisone. "I am not gaining fifty pounds," I proclaimed. Apparently, my body listened and I didn't.

Some words are spoken aloud; others are said to ourselves silently as thoughts. In terms of alignment words are like the God Janus, they face inwards and outwards at once. Words do two things: they reveal what is going on inwardly in our thoughts and feelings, and words can be used outwardly to redirect our thoughts.

We can purposely use our words to create new thoughts that will lead to different feelings, actions, and results.

Listen closely to a person and they will give you clues about what is going on inside them. Listen closely to yourself and to what you say. Rasputin said, "It is impossible to keep a secret because we leak disclosure from every pore."

"I have a huge list to get done today," I once said to a friend.

"You mean a long list?" my friend countered.

"No. I mean huge."

Huge implies size and size is relational. A mountain is huge compared with a molehill. A molehill is huge compared with a speck of dust. A list might be huge in relation to what, if not the person who is representing it that way. My list did feel huge, and I felt small. My words leaked my misaligned belief of feeling inadequate.

How many times have you heard people refer to their children as 'my children' or 'your children' rather than 'our children?' What does that mean?

I once asked someone in earnest, "You mean your husband is the step-father?"

"No," she replied. "He doesn't interact with them. I'm the one that does everything, so they're mine."

I empathized with her frustration, yet it seemed she was further communicating to the father that he was to remain excluded because the children were not 'his' children, after all. They belonged to the wife.

71

Words can also leak lack of commitment in taking action. "I think I will go to bed early tonight." "Maybe I will get up extra early tomorrow." "I will try to call you later." "Perhaps I'll have this project done next week."

When we use words like try, maybe, or perhaps we are leaking something. Maybe we lack confidence in our ability to do the task. Maybe we are making a feigned commitment because it sounds nice and we are trying to please someone. Whatever the reason, there is one. There is a belief or a feeling that is in the way of simply saying, "I will" or "I won't." These are examples of how words leak our thoughts and feelings.

Words can also be used on the outside to redirect our thoughts and feelings. When I was in college, I gave a lot of riding lessons to kids. The first time they went from a walk to a trot was normally a scary moment for them and sometimes was a scary moment for me, too, while watching. They would often bounce to the right, bounce to the left, and somehow bounce themselves back to center without falling off.

"Phew!" I'd think silently to myself, but to them I'd say, "Well done! You were wonderful!" They would generally look at me with a puzzled look on their face.

"You bounced quite a bit and then you found your balance. That is exactly right! Next time will be easier. Would you like to try again?" They would. I had learned how important words are to a student's confidence. As long as they had confidence, they were willing to continue and with practice, they'd improve.

I was in high school when I was riding with a nine year old girl whose pony suddenly went racing off with her. All I could do was pace my horse a reasonable distance back so as not to further spook the pony and yell, "Lean back," hoping she would not fall off.

The pony stopped before crossing a bridge and the normally confident child was bawling.

My mind raced with words I could have said to her, "Oh my God! How terrified you must be! That was horrific to watch. I thought you were going to die!" but instead different words burst forth from my lips before I could stop them.

"You were magnificent! That was amazing! You are brilliant! How did you do that?"

"What?" she said to me bewildered. I was a bit bewildered myself but the words just kept coming.

"Your pony was running like crazy but you stopped him. I saw you pull him in. How did you do that?"

"I just kept pulling," she said.

"Well it worked. Do you think you could stop him again?"

She thought about it. "Yeah, I think I could."

"I'm impressed. You did great."

"Thank you," she said. We rode on and the girl continued riding happily for many years to come.

Words that have a negative effect on our thoughts, feelings, and abilities is just as possible. This time I was the student.

An accomplished rider was in town who was said to be on her way to the Olympics. It was a special treat to have a lesson with her. I borrowed my instructor's horse, Spot, so as to have a horse with high ability for the special occasion. We rounded a turn and were going to jump the "Trepidation," a massive fence made of two large tree trunks suspended in the air with a sizeable spread. The name of the jump said it all.

The take off was important so as to have enough scope to make the width. It was an intimidating fence, but Spot was experienced. I hung on, and true to history, Spot leaped it. Taa-daa!

I rode up to the instructor, smiling, and out of breath.

"That was terrible," she said. "Do it again."

"Uh-oh," I thought to myself as we approached it a second time. I was trying to rate the approach. "Go, no wait, no go, no wait." I couldn't find the distance. Spot didn't mind. Somehow, he managed to pick his own take off. I hung on and he leaped it again. I rode up to the instructor for my tongue lashing.

"That was just horrible! Riding like that is going to get you hurt."

We moved onto the "Giant's Chair," another large fence that was a bench with a seat and back rest, large enough for a giant. It was a strange looking fence, easier to jump than the Trepidation, but none the less, not easy.

With every jump the comments got worse and with every comment, my abilities got worse until poor Spot began refusing fences. The instructor told me to get off

74

and she got on, spanking Spot over the jumps. I remember leading Spot in, apologizing to him, feeling emotionally wrecked from the experience. I'm not the best rider in the world, but I'm not the worst rider in the world either. I had completely lost confidence which annihilated my ability to make decisions and perform.

So we can use words to have the best chance possible of generating positive results, and words can also pollute the environment and negatively influence results. Words plant the seeds for outcomes.

When words align with self, like, "I am capable. I can do this," words hold power. When words come from misaligned beliefs, "I am horrible. I can't do this," they hold power, too. It all depends on which part of ourselves we wish to empower, our true self or our misaligned beliefs.

Japanese scientist, Masaru Emoto made an interesting discovery while researching water and water pollution. He discovered that the health of water is susceptible to words and music. Water is a natural conductor of energy. Dr. Emoto discovered that when water is exposed to positive words, it forms beautiful crystals that look like snowflakes. When water is exposed to negative words, the water looks more like shapeless puddles. If you've never seen this for yourself, you might enjoy looking it up on the internet. The changes to the water are truly astonishing.

Just as our bodies contain an energy or life force that some call, Chi, Dr. Emoto calls the energy contained in words, Hado. He believes it is the hado in words that we are feeling when loving words bring a sense of comfort and destructive words cause us pain. Our bodies are something close to 70% water.

After the assassination of Martin Luther King, third grade teacher, Jane Elliott, gave her students a unique lesson in discrimination. For the first day, she told the class that the blue eyed kids were better than the kids with brown eyes. The second day, she told the class that she had lied and the brown eyed kids were better than the blue eyed ones.

The results of the lesson were startling. Not only did the children's behavior change based on what they believed, but their test scores did as well. The group that was 'superior' for the day had higher test scores than normal. The group that was' lower' for the day had lower test scores than their norm. The only thing that was different from one day to the next was which group of kids were told they were better. This lesson has been duplicated time and again with both children and adults with similar findings each time.

Words have the capacity to hold serious power and, if we are mindful of the serious power within our words, we can make declarations and fulfill them. Business contracts are agreements made by words backed up with action. Marriage vows are agreements made by the words, "I do," backed up with action. America became its own nation based on the words we call, "The Declaration of

Independence." We declared our independence, and backed it up with action.

We can use words to help realign the misaligned beliefs and anchor us back to our selves. We can use the two most powerful words in the English language, "I am."

"I will be there on time because I am accountable." "I will take the trash out because I am reliable." "I will take the new job because I am capable." "I will solve this problem because I can."

I used this strategy when I needed to paint a room in my house and have it ready by the end of the weekend. It was covered in old peeling wall paper. As I peeled the paper down, it brought chunks of the wall down with it. "I'll never get this done," I kept hearing myself say. Then I remembered to use my words to redirect my thinking.

"I am a capable, resourceful woman and painting is so simple, a monkey could do it." The thought of a monkey with a paint brush making an even bigger mess than I was making, lightened my mood.

Every time I ran into not knowing how to proceed, I reminded myself that I am a capable, resourceful woman. With each new problem to solve, I used my resourcefulness, called the hardware store, got instructions, and kept moving. By Monday morning, the room was sparkling and ready to go. "I AM a capable, resourceful woman!" I heard the soul's voice answer from deep within, "Yes, you are."

Misaligned beliefs say, "I have to... I should... I need to... I can't... because I am weak, dumb, undeserving, etc." The soul says, "I can, I choose to, I want to, I get to... because I am capable, responsible, resourceful, worthy, valuable, and strong."

Think of the brain like a little card catalog. We store memories according to the words we use and we can use our words to shape our experience. Think of the last time you had a really great day. If you had labeled that day as just an ok day, it would be located in the 'ok ' file but because you labeled it a great day, that day will always pull up when you search in your "great day" file.

When my private practice got extremely busy and full, I got behind on the paperwork and insurance billing. With every phone call for more work, I felt more and more overwhelmed and stressed out. I kept calling these events overwhelming and storing them in my 'overwhelm' file. Then I learned I could change the word and change my experience.

What if I had so many phone calls to return because I was in demand? Suddenly, I felt successful! I had a new word with which to categorize my experience and a much more joyful feeling as a result. I was in demand! How terrific was that!

We can use words to label other experiences as well. If doing dishes is slow and tedious, we will have the experience of slow and tedious every time we think of doing dishes. If doing dishes is quick and easy, we will experience a sense of quick and easy when thinking of and doing the task.

Our perception of time flies when we're having fun and drags along when we're not. If you are feeling overwhelmed, try changing the label to something better. By consciously choosing our words, we can consciously affect our state. Earl Nightingale said, "The strangest secret in the world is that you become what you think about."

Consider these two sayings: "In the beginning was the Word, and the Word was with God, and the Word was God," and "Sticks and stones may break my bones but words can never hurt me." One holds words as having the highest power possible while the other holds words as rather meaningless. Which saying is true? Might they both be true depending on how we treat our word?

It's important to be mindful of any promises we make before actually making them. If the word given is not in alignment with our self, we will position ourselves to act against our self every time we try to keep our misaligned word. If you find yourself breaking your word consistently, notice if the word you are giving is actually something that does not align with what you truly want.

I remember feeling guilty turning down simple invitations. I would either generate reasons I could not go or I would agree to go and then wish I had never made the agreement. Suddenly, I'd put myself in the position of either violating my word to someone else or violating my true desire. When the word given is in violation of our greater truth, it creates automatic inner conflict.

If we are in conflict with ourselves, we are prone to show up late, get sick, or have some other mishap as a way of avoidance. Not only that, but we predispose ourselves to resent the person we gave our word to as if they are somehow responsible for the fact that we didn't tell the truth. Purposely or not, when we are not true to our self, we set ourselves up to be untrue to others. Lip service destroys trust with other people and it erodes confidence in ourselves.

So why might we sometimes say things we don't mean? We say things we don't mean when we align our words with misaligned beliefs. Most people say, "I agree to things I don't want to do because I don't want to be mean."

Is it mean to be honest or more mean to be dishonest? Misaligned beliefs can be sneaky and to be in alignment, we must align each block with the foundation block of who we really are.

When we say no when we mean no, and yes when we mean yes, rather than disappointing others, people learn that they can trust us. We build trust with others and build esteem with our self. When congruity between words and actions is missing, we destroy trust with others and our self-esteem is eroded.

Words that are not followed by action send a mixed signal. The words say one thing but the actions say something different. Which do we believe? In the next chapter, we will be reminded to believe neither one. Instead we can realize that a person is either in alignment

80

with who they really are, or they are out of alignment with who they are which usually stems from a misaligned belief.

Before putting all the blocks together, we will move to the final block which holds all the rest of the blocks in place. The final block in the alignment process is actions.

7

ACTIONS

"The rainbows in our lives begin at our feet. To reach the desired pot of gold, large or small, we must take that first step."
Joe Palmer

My friend and colleague, Joe Palmer, and I conduct a leadership workshop for at-risk teens called the Torch Training. Joe often asks, "What time is it?" The correct answer is, "Right now!"

The training encourages a sense of urgency and poses the question, "What are you waiting for?" If you want to be close to your family, be close now. If you want to take school seriously, take school seriously now. If you are willing to stand for your greatness, stand for your greatness now. "If it's to be, it's up to…. me!" is the motto of the Torch.

ACTIONS

No one can live our lives for us and the window of opportunity does not stay open forever. Opportunities that are here today, may or may not be here tomorrow; and there is no golden rule as to how much time each one of us has. We are here as long as we are. That's it. Our loved ones are here as long as they are until they are gone as well. What are we doing with the time that we have?

On a family vacation a few years ago, I found a perfect birthday card for my mother. It said everything I had never found the words to express myself about what an amazing woman she is and how much she means to me. It was October and her birthday is in December.

I was thinking to myself, I should really give her this card right this minute because we never know what the future holds. Then my mind chatter started up, "No, wait until her birthday. You will never find another card as good as this one. Save it for her birthday." I gave into the mind chatter and held onto the card.

The next day, my mom went boating with some family members and to make a long story short, the boat they were on collided with a much larger boat, a barge. In that moment, my mom believed they were all going to die. To this day, she feels it was divine intervention that they lived.

When my mom came home, shaken and tearful, and told the story, I retrieved the card. I felt like such an idiot for not having given it to her the moment I'd bought it. I knew better. This lesson I'd been given already and I'd ignored what I'd learned from my own near death experience.

Back then, I'd always wanted a fish tank. I found an old one in the garage, filled it with water, and put fish in it. It turned green, but I had my fish tank. I wanted a garden. My mom tilled the dirt for me. The gophers sucked the watermelon plants under the ground the first day, but I planted my garden.

When I got home from the bone marrow biopsy, I nailed together a flower box, put it outside my bedroom window, and filled it with my favorite flowers. I needed to see things growing. When a friend invited me to go paragliding, I said yes. After a three minute lesson, I strapped a parachute to my back, jumped off a mountain, and I was flying.

When I learned my hair would fall out, I decided to cut it and since I'd had long hair my whole life, I decided to take photos to make the occasion memorable. I grabbed Lucero, the horse I'd been riding, grabbed my old prom dress, and my mom grabbed her camera.

There was no bath for the horse, no plans as to lighting, no idea what the tide conditions would be, or the angle of the sun. We pinned the dress on with safety pins because I'd lost so much weight, the dress was too big. I climbed on Lucero bareback when I have always used a saddle, kicked off my shoes, and we were off. None of the usual preparation stuff mattered. We decided to do it. We did it, and it was done.

ACTIONS

These things happened in days, not weeks. Action was easy. There was nothing in the way to hinder the results. If it was going to happen, it got to happen right now, as in today. No excuses and no second guessing. It was an important lesson in how effortless action can be when the mind chatter is not in the way.

For alignment, action is the final step. Alignment has its foundation in the self but it is achieved through action. "Self-actualization" is getting the self to show up on the outside. In the end, we can think it, we can feel it, we can say it, but it's not until we do it that it's done.

Paying attention to someone's actions can give you a lot of information. Just like words, actions either align with the true self or they align with misaligned beliefs. By having an understanding of how misaligned beliefs operate, actions that don't seem to make sense initially, can be read differently and suddenly make sense in a misaligned way. Actions reveal what we are subconsciously most committed to and sometimes subconsciously, we are most committed to our misaligned beliefs.

To learn what you are most committed to, take a hard, honest look at your actions. Let's use being late as a simplistic example since so many of us can relate with being late.

When you are late, what is more important to you than being on time? Think about it. When we're late, we are making something else a higher value. Maybe it's sleeping a little longer or getting one more thing done before we leave the house. Maybe being late is a way of sabotaging our success. Maybe we enjoy the sense of self-importance we get by having other people wait around for us.

For me, I used to value getting one more thing done before leaving the house. Because I used to believe that there was always something I should be doing, just as it was time to leave, I would throw a load of clothes in the washing machine or decide I needed to take out the trash on the way out the door.

I was making that one last thing more important than being on time, but more than that, I was making that one last thing more important than feeling calm during my drive. The ironic part is that I was squeezing that last task in, in order to feel calmer but instead of causing me to feel more on top of things, putting too much into too small a space was actually increasing my stress. Once I figured that out, I stopped doing it.

Just consider for a moment, when you are late, what are you making more important than being on time? Any time we say one thing yet do another, we are committed to something other than what we've said.

If you are trying to get in better shape but are chronically missing your workouts, something else is a higher priority than getting in shape. If you are trying to complete a project but find yourself procrastinating, something else is a higher priority to you.

Inaction is also an action. What are we committed to when we are avoiding, stuck, or procrastinating?

ACTIONS

A study was done with animals. An animal was put in a cage and received shocks every time it stepped in a specific area. The animal soon learned where it was safe to move and which areas to avoid. The animal moved around the cage, taking specific actions and avoiding specific others.

Another poor little animal was put in a cage and shocked at random. There were no designated shock areas or safe zones. This animal could not predict where movement was safe and where it was harmful.

Eventually, this animal stopped moving around entirely. It cowered in a corner in an attempt to avoid pain it could not learn to predict. Scientists have named this condition, "learned helplessness."

When we find ourselves avoiding action, it is likely that we are anticipating some sort of fear or discomfort associated with taking the action. All mammals instinctively avoid pain. All mammals naturally move away from discomfort and move toward perceived comfort.

Even positive outcomes that are unfamiliar can cause a sense of discomfort. If we aren't certain what success will bring, we may avoid being successful. This creates the set up for self-sabotage.

Self-sabotage is often at play when a person's words and actions don't match. It doesn't mean that a person is a good person or a bad person if they say one thing and do another. It is more likely, that their actions are aligning with some deeply held belief as in the example of the man who kept causing problems with his girlfriend when things got to be too good. "I thought that being with you was too good to be true," he shared. We each have an internal blue print for our comfort zone in life. Anything that gets too far from that blueprint, even when it's positive, can be a trigger to shift behavior and bring us back to the status quo.

Every time we take an action that aligns with our true self, our self esteem gets stronger and the alignment of all five blocks will get straighter. Every time our actions align with misaligned beliefs, those false beliefs will gets stronger and we will get more misaligned. The challenge is to stop taking actions that prove the wrong beliefs right, and to instead, do what it takes to be you.

In the beginning, taking action that goes against misaligned beliefs may be extremely difficult. The misaligned beliefs will scream, challenge, push, prod, shame, manipulate, lie, induce guilt, create fear, and do all they can to cause you to let yourself down.

If I have learned a single thing in life, however, it is that any time we follow our gut, do what is in our heart, and do what we know is right for us, our soul never, ever, gets it wrong not even once. The ending may turn out ugly, painful, or messy but it will always turn out honest, true, and in integrity. For better or worse, we don't tend to feel regret when we've acted in integrity with ourselves.

It is the anticipation of action that generally holds the dread. Actions themselves, once accepted and broken down into small steps, are generally quite simple. The point of power is always in the present moment. The Zen warriors say, "Be here now." The good news is, we can condition our actions just like we can condition our muscles.

With repetition, taking action tends to become easier over time. Any task we do in a repetitive way can become almost automatic once it gets conditioned like a habit, into our neuro-pathways.

In school, I remember drawing the letter A over and over again, page after page, when I was first learning how to write. Holding the pencil felt awkward. Today, not only can I write; I can type. Now it's easy, but when I first began, it felt hard.

Generally speaking, actions becomes easier with practice regardless of how difficult they feel at first. The pilot eventually learns to fly the plane, the surgeon eventually learns to perform surgery, the bull rider eventually learns to ride the bull.

Every summer, since 1992, my mom and I have been taking a hiking trip. The first year, we hiked up Half Dome in Yosemite. We've been to nearly every one of the Channel Islands off the Santa Barbara coast, and we've hiked up Mt. Whitney twice.

Our trips are always one day excursions, affectionately known as hikes from hell. We get up early in the morning, start walking, and we don't stop until we make our destination. We've left, sometimes, at five am, and returned in the wee hours of two or three the next morning. We've come in with black toenails and blisters, but the one thing we never do is stop.

We get tired, we get hot, we get cold, and we get grumpy but as long as we keep going, we always arrive at our destination eventually. One thing I've learned from hiking is that sometimes you have no idea how close you are to reaching your destination until you round the last curve. All of the sudden what felt like it would never come, is suddenly right before your eyes.

The same is true with life. If we just keep going, don't stop, don't quit, and don't give up, eventually we will get where we want to be. Persistence is the key.

There is always a result to taking action and those results can create evidence to support accurate beliefs about who we are. If we do something that helps someone, it's easy to identify ourselves as helpful. If we do something kind, it's easy to acknowledge the kindness within us.

It's important to note, however, that the results of our actions are not always within our immediate control and even when we take aligned action, our results may or may not be what we ultimately wanted. It is important to not judge yourself overly harshly if your actions do not generate your desired results. Instead, shift yourself, change something, and try again. There is no such thing as failure, only feedback.

Michelangelo said, "The greater danger for most of us is not that our aim is too high and we miss it but that it is too low and we reach it." We cannot control every outcome.

Instead, we can do our best to keep our actions aligned with our highest values, aim high, and rather than beating ourselves up for an unwanted result, we can acknowledge ourselves for our effort.

When our actions align with our self, every block of ourselves becomes straighter. Actions are the locking pin for alignment.

8

PUTTING IT ALL TOGETHER

"It takes a lifetime to live a lifetime." -Ray Hunt

It's hard to believe it's been eighteen years since the day I galloped Lucero down the beach. In hindsight, the whole experience was one of the best things that could have ever happened to me. It taught me many things and it brought me to myself.

For me, the message was, " Be real. Be who you are. Limits are illusions. What other people think doesn't matter. What you think of yourself does. You may feel alone but there is a wisdom that will guide you if you learn to listen. You can utilize yourself and your life."

It taught me that it's possible to live aligned with my true nature. It showed me my greatness, and exposed to me that greatness is in everyone. I know now, we are each powerful and special beyond measure. At our core, each one of us is sacred.

Life is a journey. In the words of Ray Hunt, "It takes a lifetime to live a lifetime." The secret to happiness is to be ourselves, live on purpose, and express our own uniqueness. With time and practice, who we are on the inside will become more and more visible on the outside. Our lives will become a greater reflection of who we are.

We are not just one part; we are many parts that come together to act in unison. Each person is heart, spirit, and soul. Each person is born whole and complete in spirit. Our spirit, soul, or self is the foundation of alignment.

As we grow, we make meaning about ourselves, others, and our world. When our beliefs align with our self, we tend to feel good. When our beliefs align with other people's judgments and opinions more than our own, it creates inner conflict. Most often, it is in our beliefs that misalignment begins.

Feelings tend to follow thoughts. Feelings are real, yet they tend to be based on our interpretations which may, or may not, be accurate. Feelings are like a flashing red light at an intersection saying, "Hey, pay attention here." If we are feeling peaceful and content, chances are we are in alignment. If we are feeling anxious, depressed, or doubtful, chances are we are misaligned.

Words reveal outwardly what is going on inwardly in our thoughts and in our feelings. Words can be used to set a course and keep us on track.

And finally, actions reveal what we are most committed to at any given time, primarily our self or our misaligned beliefs. Actions create evidence that either strengthens our self-esteem or weakens it. Every action that aligns with the foundation of who we are, pulls our blocks straighter and strengthens self- confidence. The locking pin for alignment is action that aligns with self.

Life is not fixed and we are not fixed. Because life is in constant motion, circumstances will likely knock us out of alignment. Achieving balance takes constant readjustment, sometimes on a moment to moment basis. The encouraging part is that once we learn the concepts behind alignment, we have the ability to identify which part or parts to readjust. How and where to make adjustments becomes easier and easier to recognize.

A friend of mine is exceptionally beautiful. She has long, thick hair and a dazzling smile. People remark often about her beauty which used to cause her to feel terribly uncomfortable.

My friend was beautiful according to society's values, but acknowledging her appearance accurately caused her to feel extremely uncomfortable. She felt awkward, embarrassed, and sad when people would comment on her beauty.

"I am ugly," she would say. Her words revealed her thoughts.

'Ugly?,' I thought. How could she not see her beauty? Then one day, my friend opened up to me. "I was molested as a child. I hate how I look. I hate my body. I can't stand to see myself. I am so ugly."

In time, my friend challenged her beliefs and realigned her thinking. "Being molested was an experience that I had but it does not define who I am. Now when people compliment me, it feels good to simply say, 'Thank you,' and feel good about who I am."

In terms of alignment, change can happen quickly and it can also happen slowly. Most often, change happens in increments and adds up over time. There is no right or wrong time line and no right or wrong method. It takes the time it takes and inches are miles.

Without understanding alignment, there may be temptation to judge others and misjudge ourselves. Alignment is not a tool to judge; instead it gives us the ability to have deeper understanding, and hopefully, greater compassion. One of the best ways to help each other and ourselves is to remember that each of us is a soul experiencing a sometimes turbulent life. We don't always make logical sense. Bumps, bruises, and scars are not the real person. Grumbling words, broken promises, and bad attitudes are not each person either. People are faulty, we make mistakes, try hard, do our best, and fall short sometimes. We are each affected by the history of our lives.

The greatest gift we can give one another is to simply recognize that each of us is a soul and spirit doing the best we know how to do at any given time. Regardless of what people say or don't say, and regardless of what people do or don't do, we can treat one another as the soul and spirit we each are.

Maryanne Williamson said it so well, "Our deepest fear is not that we are inadequate. Our deepest fear is that we are powerful beyond measure. It is our light, not our darkness, that frightens us most. We ask ourselves, 'Who am I to be brilliant, gorgeous, talented, and famous?' Actually, who are you not to be? You are a child of God. Your playing small does not serve the world. There is nothing enlightened about shrinking so that people won't feel insecure around you. We were born to make manifest the glory of God that is within us. It's not just in some of us; it's in all of us. And when we let our own light shine, we unconsciously give other people permission to do the same. As we are liberated from our own fear, our presence automatically liberates others."

So, who are you, dear reader? Are you a loving, capable, and intelligent woman? Are you an honorable, caring, and joyful man? This world is the canvas. You decide. You have the seed to every quality within you already, and you are magnificent whether you know it or not.

Best wishes and good luck,

Faith

About The Author

Faith Deeter, MFT is a Licensed Therapist , coach, trainer, and speaker. She is the founder of Galloping Thru Life Therapeutic Riding Program, and a trainer for The Torch Foundation providing leadership workshops for at-risk youth. Her work has been featured on numerous radio programs and print publications.

ALSO BY FAITH DEETER

- The Conflict Pattern Revealed: See the Pattern, Stop the Fight, and have Happier Relationships Now

- Contributing author of:
    Thank God I... Book 3
    "Finding Faith"

www.ingramcontent.com/pod-product-compliance
Lightning Source LLC
LaVergne TN
LVHW021525080426
835509LV00018B/2675